Algorithmic Invisibility

ON THE INPUT GAP OF THE DIGITALIZED WORLD

Algorithmic Invisibility

Understanding the Threat and the Strategy to Overcome It

DREY RUSSELL

Always On Press · 2026

Published by Always On Press
alwaysonmarketing.co

ISBN 979-8-9959206-1-8 (Paperback)

First edition, 2026
Printed in the United States of America

Contents

Preface 9

Chapter 1 — What is Algorithmic Invisibility 13

Chapter 2 — Narrative Engineering 17

Chapter 3 — SEO is Dead. Welcome to GEO. 21

Chapter 4 — The 15 Signs of Invisibility 27

Chapter 5 — Distinguishing the Four Types of Work 31

Chapter 6 — The Operational Audit 37

Chapter 7 — The Presence Economy 41

Closing — A Final Note 47

About the Author 49

Bibliography 51

"That grey space in the middle is what the 21st century is going to be about."

— David Bowie, BBC Newsnight, 1999

PREFACE

Why I Wrote This

The world you know is currently disappearing, rendered invisible by the layered infrastructures of data and algorithms. It is a matter of input: the work of rendering the physical world legible to the digital world remains largely undone.

We once viewed the internet as a window to the world. Today, however, we discovered that the digital infrastructure operates as a restrictive interface that curates reality for us, a selective lens that prioritizes what is processable and indexable over what is inherently local, physical or true.

This means, we are losing access to our surroundings not because they have ceased to exist, but because the touchpoints of our perception have been reconfigured by the AI's new parameters of visibility — a system that fails to account for the unpredictable nature of the physical environment. The result is a landscape where the territory remains geographically intact, but informational access to it has been fragmented.

This structural level is compounded by a barrier of convenience: while digital environments optimize for immediate, domestic consumption, physical movement requires a cost of decision — in time, effort, and resources — that many are increasingly unwilling to pay. A place or community may persist on a geographic plane, yet it loses its social viability as digital inertia replaces the impulse for presence.

The central structure of this book originated in a master's research project focused on the architecture of digital social networks. For over a decade, I have been investigating audience behavior within the digital sphere, mapping how mediatization and datafication have transformed the processes of discovery, understanding, orientation, and the formation of collectivities.

I sought to understand a specific friction: why communities become inaccessible from the outside — sealed not by physical walls, but by layers of algorithmic curation, social reinforcement, and shared identity. These layers accumulate until the membrane becomes effectively impenetrable, creating what we traditionally identified as bubbles or clusters.

Between 2023 and 2026, the way we interact with the world changed completely. However, what was observed was not a rupture with the past, but rather a systemic progression of the very same phenomenon. The filter solidified into an architecture, while the scope of what remains beyond our digital reach expanded. The result is what we call “algorithmic invisibility.”

After developing this thought, I came to the United States. I found here a rich scenario to better understand the interlocking forces I had mapped in my research (technology, social patterns, content, and identity), and its impact in day to day life beyond the theoretical point of view. The environment inspired me to pivot from pure research to practical application: a methodology engineered to those that thrive on physical experience and engagement beyond the digital interface — communities as well as businesses.

My aim is to help people to navigate the AI’s new parameters of visibility and convert digital interest into real decisions — gathering people online and off.

This approach is designed for leadership for whom algorithmic invisibility is not merely a commercial challenge, it is an existential risk. When the audience is removed from these physical institutions, the entity does not merely diminish; it ceases to exist.

What you will find in these pages

What follows is a strategic framework, a practical guide, designed for those who recognize that the digital shift has fundamentally altered our relationship with reality. This book translates a decade of investigation into a practical methodology for anyone seeking to reclaim visibility — whether for their businesses, their institutions, their communities, or their own personal autonomy.

You will find:

• A quick definition of what Algorithmic Invisibility is and how it operates.

• An honest account of why the problem is not merely communication — and what kind of work needs to be done.

• The vocabulary you need to navigate the new landscape of AI-mediated discovery — including what GEO is, what a Digital Twin is, what Phygital means in practice.

• The fifteen signs that indicate invisibility, grouped by the layer of the membrane where the invisibility lives.

• A framework that connects each layer of invisibility to a distinct kind of corrective work — with honest horizons for each.

• A self-audit you can do on your own, today, with no tools beyond a browser and a notepad.

• And finally, a framework I have been calling the Presence Economy — a way of thinking about what is on the other side of the current noise.

I wrote this because the conversation around Artificial Intelligence and Algorithms has drifted too far from the ground. It has become a distant debate, detached from the practical reality of our society. I wanted to close that gap. I wanted to make the process legible and provide the tools for people to orient themselves and seek improvement.

— Drey Russell · Journalist, researcher, media strategist · April 2026

CHAPTER ONE

What is Algorithmic Invisibility

In 2024, AI search was an early signal. In 2025, it became a trend. In early 2026, it is a structural reality that is changing those that appear and who won't — the numbers tell the story plainly.

The pace of adoption across generative platforms like ChatGPT, Gemini, and Perplexity has been exponential, with active user counts accelerating past 700 million users in early 2026. This rapid shift has led leading analysts, such as Gartner, to project that traditional search engine volume will drop significantly — potentially by 25% by the end of 2026, as AI chatbots capture that share.

What this means in practice: when someone asks "What's a good Italian restaurant for my in-laws' anniversary near me?" — they are increasingly not typing that into Google anymore. They are asking ChatGPT. Or Perplexity. Or the AI Overview that Google now places above its own search results.

And that AI does not show them a list of ten restaurants to choose from. It shows them a short, synthesized answer — often naming two or three places inside a confident paragraph that reads like advice from a knowledgeable friend. The list is gone. What remains is a recommendation, and the businesses that fall outside of it are, for practical purposes, absent from the decision.

The new logic is different. The AI that now answers the customer's question is not ranking a list of restaurants. It is writing a paragraph and deciding whether to include the brand in that paragraph. The decision is made by a synthesis engine that reads across many sources and chooses whom to reference.

To be cited, a business has to exist in a form that this new engine can read, trust, and reference. That form is almost never what a conventional website or social media account provides.

The infrastructure of discovery changed, and no one talks about it.

AI recommendation systems, in aggregate, reward sources that demonstrate what the industry has started calling E-E-A-T — Experience, Expertise, Authority, and Trust. Generic content is not ignored because the engines are punitive; it is ignored because it provides the synthesis layer with nothing specific to say. For physical businesses, this means that the right keywords are no longer enough. Authority and structured data have become the minimum.

The four levels approach

I described the fundamental architecture through which we perceive reality — the filtered informational clusters in which most of us now live online — as a membrane that operates on four levels at once: technological, social, content and identity. To break through such a membrane you have to address all four:

The technological level. The algorithms that curate what you see, the AI systems that decide which sources to cite, the APIs that govern what moves between platforms.

The social level. The patterns of interaction, the accumulated social capital, the habitus — the inherited way of being in the world — that determines which people, and therefore which businesses, get amplified and which get filtered out.

The content level. The specific formats, structures, and languages that the network has learned to recognize as worth circulating. Content that does not match these formats becomes invisible even when it is excellent.

The identity level. The way bubbles reinforce who belongs and who does not, creating insulated communities where certain businesses are mentioned constantly and others are never spoken of at all.

In the context of this book, I will refer to the 'content' layer as 'narrative' to reflect the specific form this layer takes when the object on the outside of the membrane is a physical business rather than a journalistic source. The mechanism is the same; the register has shifted.

If you only think about this phenomenon as a technological issue, or only about content, you will fail. The infrastructure does not merely filter what enters. It renders what is outside it invisible. Not hidden. Not suppressed. Simply absent from the conversation — as though it never existed.

The four forms of invisibility

Algorithmic invisibility is the structural progression of the fragmentation. It is the result of what began as a filter that has hardened into an architecture over the years. My assumption is that the scope of what remains outside now has expanded. It is no longer only dissenting viewpoints or specific data points that disappear. It is the physical world itself.

1. Structural invisibility. The information exists online — but in a form that AI engines cannot parse cleanly. Hours are in an image instead of text. The menu is a PDF instead of a structured page. The address is formatted differently on three different platforms. The AI cannot be confident about what is true, so it omits the business.

2. Narrative invisibility. The digital ecosystem is managed without a unified narrative strategy. Social media is handled by one department, the website by another, and directory listings by a third. The result is an incoherent Digital Twin: a signal so fragmented that the system cannot form a reliable picture.

3. Social invisibility. The business is parseable and has a narrative — but it does not appear in the specific formats and social platforms AI draws from for training and retrieval (long-form editorial, curated directories, community discourse). It is not on Reddit. Its Instagram has a few hundred followers because the algorithm never served it to anyone.

4. Identity invisibility. This is the deepest layer. Even with readable information, growing social capital, and well-structured content, a business can remain invisible if it lacks a story attached to it; if it has not been admitted into the cultural conversation that defines its category. Belonging is earned through presence in the sources, communities, and cultural registers that constitute the category.

Algorithmic invisibility is not a failure of quality. Not a failure of effort. But a structural condition that needs to be addressed on all four levels, coherently, with intent.

The four-pillar framework that follows — adapted from my master's research — provides the analytical structure for resolving algorithmic invisibility, and the rest of this book walks through each pillar in turn: first the diagnosis (Chapter 4), then the kinds of work each one requires (Chapter 5), then the operational audit (Chapter 6), then the presence economy (Chapter 7).

CHAPTER TWO

Narrative Engineering

Conventional marketing will not resolve algorithmic invisibility; nor will digital marketing. Both operate on the assumption that the problem is merely communication. It is not.

The problem is structural in its core. Resolving algorithmic invisibility requires knowledge from other pragmatic-oriented disciplines, such as engineering.

Engineering is the practice of diagnosing a system's structure before intervening in it. An engineer does not guess. An engineer maps the structure, identifies where it fails, and applies the specific intervention the failure requires. And because the final output of the work is always the way a place appears in the cultural conversation — the story that gets told about it — the specific form of engineering this book proposes has a name: Narrative Engineering.

While standard agencies were posting on behalf of their clients, the attention economy was collapsing around them. Consumers aren't just scrolling past content. They're actively rejecting advertising as a category. The agencies responded to declining attention by spending more. More posts. More ads. More budget. But the problem was never volume. The problem was relevance. Digital marketing offered plumbing when businesses needed Narrative Engineering.

Narrative Engineering is the strategic architecture designed to dissolve the four layers of invisibility — technological, social, narrative, and identity — that isolate physical institutions from the contemporary digital landscape. Unlike traditional digital marketing, which interrupts to capture momentary attention, Narrative

Engineering builds a permanent structural asset rooted in the Presence Economy. It is fundamentally crossmedia, ensuring that a brand is coherent, authoritative, and irreplaceable across every touchpoint.

What makes it engineering, and not craftsmanship, is the insistence on diagnosis before intervention, on replicable principles rather than intuition. The word narrative remains central because the final product of the work is always a reconstituted story — the way a place appears in the cultural conversation.

Why the plumbing didn't fit

Almost every agency has sold digital marketing while calling it marketing. Part of what makes this conversation hard is that different disciplines have been sold under the same label.

Marketing is the art of understanding whom a brand serves, what that audience needs, and how to communicate the value of what is offered. It is a timeless and essentially strategic discipline.

Traditional Marketing (Strategic): Focuses on building Narrative Authority and on the long-term relationship between the organization and its community. It operates according to the logic of the Presence Economy, wherein the objective is to be the trusted solution for a specific human need.

Digital marketing: Is the tactical execution of marketing across digital channels — social media management, email campaigns, paid ads on Google and Meta, content scheduling. Digital marketing is plumbing. It was built for businesses whose entire relationship with the customer happens online: e-commerce, SaaS, apps, direct-to-consumer products.

Digital marketing was designed around a specific assumption: that the customer journey is a funnel that happens on screens. They see an ad. They click. They visit a site. They fill out a form. They buy. Every step is measurable, optimizable, A/B testable.

This assumption does not describe how the business actually works.

The customer's journey looks more like this: they are having a conversation with their cousin about where to take their mother for her birthday. The cousin says "I heard about a place a few towns over." Nothing more specific. That night, the person searches "best restaurant for a birthday dinner near me" in ChatGPT. They read a paragraph. They pick one of the two or three places mentioned. They make a reservation two weeks out.

In this journey, there is no ad. There is no click. There is no funnel. There is a paragraph written by a machine, read in bed, that determines a $400 dinner at a restaurant — or at its competitor.

The digital marketing agency hired has no product that addresses this journey. Their tools measure clicks. Their metrics count impressions. Their reports show improvement in things that don't matter, because the thing that matters is whether the paragraph mentioned the business.

The infrastructure they work with was built for a different kind of business. They are measuring something that has stopped being the same thing as the business growing.

The specific ways it went wrong

Here are the four most common failure modes of traditional digital marketing:

A. Content volume without narrative authority. The agency posted four times a week. The posts were on-brand. Engagement was low but steady. But none of the content created the kind of story that other websites or AI systems would reference. It was wallpaper, not a signal.

B. Paid ads for audiences that don't exist. The agency runs broad geographic targeting and reports an audience of hundreds of thousands. In reality, the customers who would love the business are a small subset — likely measured in thousands of households, not hundreds of thousands. The targeting is performative, not precise.

C. Metrics that improve while the business softens. An Instagram account grows modestly. Website traffic ticks upward. But Friday reservations are down year-over-year. The metrics improve. The business doesn't. This is the most painful failure mode, because it makes the operator feel irrational for sensing that something is wrong.

D. No one owns the digital twin. A common pattern: one agency manages Instagram. Another freelancer handles Google Business. Someone close to the owner built the website years ago. Nobody is responsible for the integrated picture of the business as it appears across the internet. The result is incoherence — hours that disagree across platforms, photos from three different eras, descriptions written in three different voices. For the AI to be confident about a brand, it needs coherence everywhere. Most businesses are coherent nowhere.

This guide is an attempt to offer a different model entirely. One that starts from the physical that has already been built and asks how the digital world can finally reflect it.

Unlike traditional digital marketing, this discipline does not focus on capturing momentary clicks; it focuses on building a permanent structural asset.

CHAPTER THREE

SEO is Dead. Welcome to GEO.

For most of the last twenty years, being found online meant one thing: appearing near the top of Google's search results. The discipline that got you there was called Search Engine Optimization — SEO. You understood its logic. Someone searches. Google shows a list. You want to be on that list, ideally near the top.

That era is ending, and something structurally different is replacing it.

What AI changed

When someone asks ChatGPT, Perplexity, Claude, or Google's AI Overview a question today, the system does not return a list of links. It returns an answer — a synthesized paragraph written by the AI, which reads across many sources and composes a coherent response that cites only a few.

In the old logic, the user would see ten results, click two or three, and form an opinion. A business had multiple chances to be seen, even if it was the sixth result. In the new logic, the user reads one paragraph that mentions two or three names. Everything outside that paragraph is invisible to the decision. The user does not scroll. They do not click. They have their answer.

This is not a small change. It is a fundamental restructuring of how businesses get discovered.

Research from Seer Interactive found that 58.5% of Google searches in the US already end without a click — rising to 75% on mobile. When AI Overviews appear, organic click-through rates drop significantly; one major study found a drop of 61% in their measured dataset. The decision is now being made inside the paragraph, not on the page the business owns.

Summary of the Transition: From Search to Answer Engines

Feature	Legacy Search (SEO)	AI-Driven (AEO)
Output Style	A list of links	A synthesized answer
Primary Metric	Click-Through Rate	Citations and Brand Mentions
Content Strategy	Keyword density and backlinks	Context, trust, and social proof
User Role	User filters and chooses	AI composes a recommendation
Goal	Visibility on first page	Becoming the "Trusted Source"

From SEO to GEO

A new discipline emerged to address this reality. It was introduced by researchers at Princeton, Georgia Tech, and the Allen Institute for AI in 2023. They called it Generative Engine Optimization — GEO.

GEO is not a replacement for SEO. It is a different discipline that works alongside it. The goal of SEO is to rank on a results page. The goal of GEO is to be cited in an AI-generated answer.

SEO asks: How high does this website rank when someone searches for its category? **GEO asks:** When an AI is asked a question the business could answer, does it mention the brand?

SEO rewards: Keyword density, technical site structure, link authority. **GEO rewards:** Semantic clarity, structured facts, verifiable statistics, narrative authority across the web.

According to Princeton's research, the top GEO methods — citing sources, adding statistics, including expert quotes —

improved AI visibility by 30 to 40% in the conditions studied. Comparison articles accounted for 32.5% of AI citations in the same research dataset. User-generated platforms like Reddit and YouTube are among the most-cited sources in AI responses observed to date.

For physical businesses, the implications are direct. The restaurant that appears when a user asks ChatGPT about “the best place for an anniversary nearby” is not necessarily the restaurant with the best SEO. It is the restaurant whose presence has been consistently established across editorial mentions, review platforms, local press, structured listings, and authoritative content that the AI has learned to trust.

The Digital Twin

Every physical business (or being) now has, whether the owner knows it or not, a digital twin. The digital twin is the version of a business that exists across the systems that mediate discovery — the Google Business Profile, the website, the Instagram feed, Yelp and TripAdvisor, mentions in local press, reviews on niche platforms, references in Reddit threads, citations in AI training data. A digital twin is assembled by these systems without any active permission. It is not optional. It exists.

The only question is whether that digital twin is as authentic as the physical original, or whether it is a diminished, incoherent ghost of it.

In many cases, the digital twin is a ghost. The photos are old. The hours are wrong on two of the seven platforms. The description was written by someone who visited once in 2019. Nobody has updated the menu on the third-party aggregators since last summer.

This ghost is what the AI is reading when it decides whether to recommend the business.

The digital twin is one of the central instruments that Narrative Engineering builds and maintains. Ensuring that a physical business has a digital twin — a version of itself in the systems that now mediate discovery — as extraordinary as the physical original is among the most concrete outputs of the discipline.

Phygital: the frame that resolves the confusion

The word is ugly. I did not invent it. But the concept it names is the most useful single idea for anyone trying to navigate the physical-business landscape of 2026.

Phygital means that the physical and the digital are no longer separate domains. They are one continuous experience of the business, and the customer does not distinguish between them. When a potential customer discovers a restaurant in an AI Overview, that is the beginning of the dining experience — not a precursor to it.

A business does not have a physical side and a digital side. It has one continuous presence that happens to move between bodies and screens. The physical side is what has always been done well. The digital side is what has been neglected — not from lack of care, but because the agencies contracted to handle it were never designed to understand the physical side deeply enough to represent it faithfully.

A phygital business, done right, feels the same in the dining room as it does in the Instagram feed as it does in the AI-generated answer. This coherence is what the AI learns to trust, what the customer learns to recognize, and what ultimately makes a physical business not only visible but inevitable.

Narrative Engineering is the discipline of building that coherence. The rest of this guide will show how to diagnose where that coherence is broken today, and what it takes to fix it before the window closes.

CHAPTER FOUR

The 15 Signs of Invisibility

The following diagnostic identifies the structural and narrative failures that lead to algorithmic invisibility. These fifteen signs appear most frequently in organizations in the physical world that are not being effectively translated into a digital twin. When applying this diagnostic, the presence of seven to ten of these markers indicates a critical disconnect from the modern infrastructure of discovery.

Signs of Structural Invisibility

1. The Brand is Unsearchable in Generative AI Tools. A primary test involves prompting ChatGPT, Perplexity, or Gemini with localized queries such as "What is the best [category] in [location]?" If the organization does not appear in the synthesized response, it is invisible to the rapidly growing segment of consumers who have moved away from traditional search lists.

2. The Google Business Profile Lacks Data Depth. A profile with fewer than 40 photos, outdated hours, or unanswered queries prevents AI engines from establishing the confidence necessary to recommend the brand.

3. The Website Lacks Structured Data (Schema Markup). Without invisible code identifying the organization's specific attributes, AI systems must infer the brand's details from surrounding context. Implementing schema markup is one of the highest-leverage structural fixes for legibility.

4. Core Information is Trapped in Images or PDFs. AI engines struggle to parse text embedded in JPEGs or beautifully designed PDF menus. When an organization's offerings are digitally illegible, they are far less likely to appear in AI recommendations, regardless of their visual elegance.

Signs of Narrative Invisibility

5. The Editorial Narrative has Stalled. AI engines draw heavily on editorial mentions from respected regional and industry publications to establish legitimacy. If a brand has not been cited in the press within the last two years, its narrative authority tends to appear "cold" to the synthesis layer.

6. The Web Presence Lacks Synthesis Material. A website limited to basic "Home" and "Contact" pages provides no narrative texture for an AI to synthesize. Cited businesses are those that provide stories about their architecture, community, and specific expertise.

7. Reviews Lack Narrative Depth. Volume matters, but synthesis engines appear to draw disproportionately on reviews that tell specific stories rather than generic praise. A handful of detailed accounts of unique experiences tends to do more narrative work than hundreds of shallow, four-star ratings.

Signs of Social Invisibility

8. Absence from Community Discourse Platforms. Reddit threads, local blogs, independent press, and video platforms (including YouTube and short-form content on platforms like TikTok) are among the most frequently cited sources in AI responses observed to date.

9. Stagnant Social Signals. A low follower count or engagement rate on platforms like Instagram often indicates that the algorithm has ceased to serve the account meaningfully. In 2026, this is evidence that the network of discovery has routed around the brand entirely.

10. Absence from Niche Category Platforms. Discovery is often mediated through specialized directories (e.g., Eater for restaurants, The Knot for venues, or Wine Enthusiast for wineries). Failure to maintain a presence on these authoritative category-specific nodes keeps the brand hidden from the sources the AI returns to when answering category questions.

11. Monolingual Limitation in Diverse Markets. In linguistically diverse regions, content that exists only in one language is inaccessible to segments of the local population who ask AI questions in another. Because AI engines respond in the user's language, businesses that publish only monolingually concede those queries entirely.

12. Diffuse Brand Identity Across Stakeholders. When internal stakeholders and regular consumers describe the brand differently, the AI will settle on the most generic description possible, placing the organization in direct competition with every other business in its category.

Signs of Identity Invisibility

13. Absence of Ritualized Community. Organizational identity is constructed through repeated rituals rather than mere transactions. Rituals — such as a decade-long recurring seminar, a specific weekend gathering of legacy members, or an annual multi-generational tradition — form the social infrastructure that constitutes a brand's true identity. Without these rhythms, there is no consistent pattern for stakeholders to name, remember, or circulate. What is repeated becomes remembered, and what is remembered eventually enters the cultural record that AI systems parse.

14. Isolation from External Discourse. An organization whose name never leaves its own walls lacks the symbolic capital required to circulate in the larger conversation of its field. Without this external validation, AI engines treat the brand as isolated, and isolated entities are rarely prioritized in synthesized recommendations for top-tier categories.

15. Absence from Institutional Memory. AI systems do not invent recommendations; they synthesize them from curated lists, industry awards, historical registries, and serious journalism. An organization that has never been "inscribed" in these records is effectively absent from the institutional memory of its own field. This absence requires the long-term work of earning recognition from the critics, curators, and journalists who maintain these repositories.

What the Diagnostic Reveals

A high score on this diagnostic does not indicate a failure of quality in the business or institution. Instead, it reveals a failure of Narrative Engineering — a structural problem where the infrastructure of discovery has changed, but the digital representation of the brand has remained stagnant.

The structural and content signs are largely fixable through a coherent strategy of presence management. The narrative and identity signs operate on a different clock: they can be started immediately, but the compounding returns accrue over time. The next chapter explains what each of these four kinds of work actually looks like.

CHAPTER FIVE

Distinguishing the Four Types of Corrective Work

The diagnostic in the previous chapter names fifteen symptoms across four layers. Narrative Engineering is the application of logical solutions to the mechanics of algorithmic invisibility. It begins with a structural diagnosis of these layers and proceeds with interventions targeted precisely where the failure occurs. The four layers do not respond to the same kind of work, at the same pace, by the same hands.

The purpose of this chapter is not to teach the execution; that is beyond the scope of any single book. The purpose is to make the architecture legible, so that anyone applying the framework can recognize what each layer requires and evaluate whether the work being done actually corresponds to the layer that needs it.

The Four Kinds of Work

Below is a compact map of the four layers, the kind of corrective work each one requires, the time horizon in which that work produces visible returns, and the signal that indicates the work is compounding as it should.

Layer	Kind of Work	Pace	Signal of Progress
Technological	Structural rebuild of the digital twin	Quick / Short-Term	AI tools retrieve accurate facts about the brand

Content / Narrative	Deposition of synthesizable material	Medium-Term	Brand begins appearing in AI answers to category queries
Social	Editorial and community cultivation	Sustained / Long-Term	External voices reference the brand without prompting
Identity	Ritual, vocabulary, and institutional inscription	Longest-Term	The brand is named in the register the category uses to describe itself

1. Structural Work: Rebuilding the Digital Twin

This is the layer on which most agencies focus when they claim to "optimize for AI." It is also the simplest of the four, which is why it is overrepresented in the market: it produces visible outputs quickly.

Structural work addresses the four signs of structural invisibility: unsearchable brand facts, Google Business Profile deficits, missing schema markup, and core information trapped in unparseable formats. The instruments here are technical: structured data schemas, photo libraries with metadata, parseable menu pages, coherent addresses and hours across every platform where the brand appears.

The horizon is short: thirty to ninety days for most businesses. The signal that the work has taken hold is that direct brand queries in AI tools return accurate, specific, and consistent information. This does not yet make the brand visible in category queries — that is the next layer — but it makes the brand legible when it is named. Structural coherence is the floor, not the ceiling.

2. Content Work: Depositing Synthesizable Material

The second kind of work addresses the three signs of narrative invisibility. The AI cannot cite material that does not exist. A brand whose digital expression consists of a homepage, a menu, and a handful of Instagram posts has deposited almost nothing for the synthesis engine to work with.

Content work is the deliberate creation of material that the synthesis layer can actually use: long-form editorial about the brand's history, philosophy, or specific expertise; structured category pages that answer the comparison queries AI engines weigh heavily; multilingual versions of core content; category-platform presence (Eater, The Knot, Wine Enthusiast, and their equivalents). This last point overlaps with the work of social visibility, since specialized directories function both as content surfaces and as community-authority signals.

The brand begins appearing in AI answers to category queries only after the synthesis engines have been trained and re-trained in cycles, and after the material itself has been discovered, indexed, and weighed against competing sources.

3. Social Work: Editorial and Community Cultivation

The third kind of work addresses the five signs of social invisibility. This is where most efforts quietly give up, because the work cannot be done by the brand alone. It requires earning the voice of others.

Social and narrative work is the cultivation of external references: editorial mentions in regional and industry publications; genuine presence in community discourse on Reddit, YouTube, and local blogs; reviews that carry narrative depth rather than generic praise; independent podcasts and newsletters that discuss the brand without being paid to.

Video content — especially short-form content that sparks community discussion and is hosted on citation-worthy platforms like YouTube and TikTok — is crucial here, as synthesis engines draw heavily on these visual and social sources.

Two common mistakes deserve naming. The first is confusing paid placements for earned authority. The second is attempting to manufacture community discourse through inauthentic posting on platforms like Reddit. These platforms treat such behavior as abuse, and the AI tools that cite them tend to weigh organic conversation more heavily than promotional activity.

4. Identity Work: Ritual, Vocabulary, and Institutional Inscription

The fourth kind of work addresses the three signs of identity invisibility, and is the most misunderstood. It is also the hardest layer to deliver, because it cannot be built from the outside alone — it has to be done with the brand, over years.

Identity work has three components. The first is ritual: the cultivation of repeating rhythms that give the community around the brand something to name, return to, and describe to others. An annual event that has taken place for ten years enters the language of the category in a way no amount of paid content can replicate.

The second component is vocabulary: the deliberate cultivation of specific language that distinguishes the brand from the generic description of its category. When stakeholders, critics, and community members converge on the same distinctive vocabulary, the synthesis layer eventually adopts that vocabulary too.

The third component is institutional inscription: the work of earning a place in the repositories the category uses to remember itself — awards, curated lists, historical registries, serious journalism. An organization that has never been inscribed in the institutional memory of its field is, in the new infrastructure, effectively absent from it.

The horizon for identity work is the longest of the four, and its returns compound over decades. The signal of progress is precise: the brand is named, by others, in the register the category itself uses to describe what it values.

Why This Matters for Leadership

The reason this architecture needs to be made explicit is that most efforts are scoped as if all four kinds of work were interchangeable. They are not.

Structural work is teachable, delegable, and fast. Content work requires editorial talent and category fluency. Social and narrative work requires the patience to earn rather than purchase. Identity work requires the rarest resource of all: the willingness to treat the brand's existence in the cultural record as seriously as its founders treated its existence in the world.

Any serious application of this framework distinguishes the four and sequences them honestly. The chapter that follows offers a self-audit anyone can run.

CHAPTER SIX

The Operational Audit

This audit can be run by anyone with a browser and a notepad. It provides a clear diagnostic of the perception gap between a physical business and its digital twin.

Part One: The AI Search Test

Open three AI tools in separate browser tabs: ChatGPT, Perplexity, and Google (where AI Overviews appear at the top of results). If you have access to Claude or Gemini, open those too.

Run the following five searches in each tool. Write down what appears.

Search 1: "What's the best [your category] in [your town]?"

Search 2: "Where should I take someone special in [your county]"

Search 3: "Best [your category] near me" (with location set to your town)

Search 4: "Hidden gems [your town]"

Search 5: "[Brand name]" — a direct brand search

For each search, note three things: Does the business appear at all? If yes, is the description accurate? If no, which competitors were mentioned instead?

By the end of this test, you will have a clear, concrete picture of the brand's AI visibility. Most businesses that do this for the first time are surprised — sometimes relieved, more often alarmed. Either reaction is valuable information.

Part Two: The Google Business Profile Audit

Open the brand's Google Business Profile. If access is unclear, search "Google Business Profile" and sign in with the email originally used to claim the listing. Check the following:

A. Photos. How many photos are there? How many were added in the last 90 days? Are they high quality? If there are fewer than 40 total photos, or if the newest photo is more than three months old, this is a priority fix.

B. Hours. Are they correct? Are holiday hours updated? A recurring pattern in negative reviews of physical businesses is some version of "arrived and they were closed."

C. Attributes. Are all relevant attributes filled in? Parking, accessibility, payment types, reservations, outdoor seating, kid-friendly, dog-friendly. Each missing attribute is a question the AI cannot answer about the brand.

D. Questions. Has anyone asked questions? Have those questions been answered? Unanswered questions are a visible signal of inattention — to the AI and to the customer reading the profile.

E. Reviews. How many reviews in the last 90 days? Are they being answered — both positive and negative? A business that does not respond to reviews is treated by the algorithm as absent.

Part Three: The Website Structure Check

Go to the website. Open it on a laptop, not a phone. Answer these questions honestly:

A. Can someone who has never heard of the business understand what it does, where it is, and what makes it different — within ten seconds of landing on the homepage?

B. Are the hours and address visible without scrolling?

C. Is the menu or service list available as text on the site — not only as a PDF or image?

D. Is there narrative content beyond the basic pages? An about section with a real story? A blog, news, or journal section with at least six posts from the last year?

E. Does the site load in under three seconds? Test it at pagespeed.web.dev.

If the answer is no to three or more of these, the website is actively contributing to invisibility, not fighting it.

Part Four: The Narrative Inventory

Make a list. Write down:

A. Every press mention of the business in the last five years, with the year and publication.

B. Every podcast, YouTube video, or TikTok that has mentioned it.

C. Every Reddit thread where it has been discussed.

D. Every guide, list, or directory (industry awards, Best Of lists, Platinum club lists, premier wedding venues, etc.) where the business is included.

If this list fits on half a page, the narrative authority is thin. AI systems rely on these signals to decide who to cite. Thin narrative equals narrow visibility.

What to do with the results

This audit produces a clear picture, but it should not be the end of the process. It is the beginning. A deficit in Part One points to structural work; a deficit in Part Three points to content work; a deficit in Part Four points to narrative work; a deficit that spans all four — and reaches into how the brand itself is named and remembered — points to identity work. Improving all four, coherently and on their respective timelines, is what transforms a physical business from invisible to inevitable.

CHAPTER SEVEN

The Presence Economy

There is a larger pattern underneath everything this book has described, and it is worth naming before we close.

For the last fifteen years, the dominant logic of digital life has been the Attention Economy. The premise was simple: human attention is scarce, and the platforms, products, and businesses that capture it most efficiently win. Every decision — the design of a feed, the length of a video, the angle of a headline — was shaped by this assumption. Success was measured by how long you could keep someone looking.

The Attention Economy produced a specific culture. Infinite scrolling. Outrage as engagement strategy. Bodies emptied into screens. A generation of founders who built wealth by designing for compulsion rather than for care.

It also produced a specific marketing orthodoxy. To sell anything, you had to interrupt. To be relevant, you had to be loud. Agencies learned this logic fluently and sold it to institutions for which it was never designed — including most of the physical places that anchor their communities.

That logic is now collapsing.

The shift underneath the shift

The rise of AI-mediated discovery is usually described as a technical transition. SEO to GEO. Search engines to generative engines. Links to citations. But underneath the technical shift is something more profound.

When a person asks an AI where to take their mother for her eightieth birthday, they are not searching in the old sense. They are asking for a recommendation — the way one might have asked a well-read friend in 1985. The AI, at that moment, is performing the oldest function in commerce: word of mouth. It is recommending who is worth trusting.

This is a quiet but enormous reversal. The Attention Economy was about capturing a user. The new logic is about earning a recommendation. Capture is a one-time event. Recommendation is a relationship the AI has with a body of evidence over time.

And this is where physical places — the kinds of places this book is about — have a structural advantage they have not yet understood.

Presence as a different kind of work

The shift this book is pointing to is not, fundamentally, a shift in tools. It is a shift in what kind of work a business or an institution needs done.

The Attention Economy required promotional work. Creating content, running ads, maintaining a feed, chasing trends. The work was episodic and defensive. You had to keep doing it because attention decays instantly. The moment you stopped, you began to disappear.

The Presence Economy requires curatorial work. It is the work of making sure that every place a business is represented — from the Google Business Profile to the Reddit thread to the local blog post to the menu listing on an aggregator site — reflects the same coherent, specific, carefully articulated truth about what the place is. The work is architectural, not episodic. You do it once, well. You maintain it quietly. And it compounds.

A place with well-constructed presence does not need to shout. It is found. When someone asks the AI "where should I take my father for his retirement dinner," the paragraph that names a particular restaurant was earned months or years earlier — by the editorial mention, by the depth of the reviews, by the structured data on the site, by the photograph taken on a November afternoon that someone posted on Reddit. That restaurant did not capture attention. It earned a recommendation.

The difference matters because presence scales differently than attention. Attention is a tax a business pays every day it wants to exist. Presence is an asset it builds once and protects.

What is at stake beyond commerce

When the digital layer of discovery stops recognizing the physical layer, something cultural is lost — not only for the businesses that disappear, but for the people who would have found them.

A country club that has been the civic anchor of a town for a hundred years may continue to exist physically while disappearing from the cultural conversation because no one taught the algorithm it was still there. A bookstore that sustained a neighborhood through three generations may close not because people stopped loving bookstores, but because the new infrastructure of recommendation never learned to mention it. A family-run winery in a small valley may lose its next generation of visitors because the paragraph that would have mentioned it was written without it.

These are not marketing outcomes. They are cultural outcomes. And they are being shaped, invisibly, by the same mechanism that is deciding which restaurants get booked on Friday night.

This is why the concept of a digital twin matters beyond the commercial case. A well-constructed digital twin is a form of cultural preservation. It is the act of making sure that a place that has real value in the physical world has equivalent representation in the systems that are now deciding which places exist in the cultural consciousness of the next generation.

The deeper question

There is a question underneath all of this that deserves to be stated plainly.

If the tools that now mediate our discovery of the world begin to recognize the physical that has always existed — restaurants that fed neighborhoods for generations, clubs that held communities together, libraries that shaped how children learned to read, rooms that refused to disappear — then something important becomes possible again. The digital does not have to be the enemy of the real. It can be, at its best, a mirror that returns the physical world's best qualities back to the people.

But if these tools continue to evolve without being taught to see the physical layer — if the infrastructure of AI recommendation consolidates around the signals it currently reads, which privilege a narrow band of businesses that happen to be well-documented online — then something else will happen. A quiet, cumulative erasure. A slow forgetting of places that never did anything wrong except fail to adapt to an infrastructure that was never explained to them.

Algorithmic invisibility is not the final state of the internet. It is the current state of a transition. The structural layer of that transition can be closed quickly; the narrative and identity layers require sustained, long-term effort, and reward those who start early. Places that matter will be visible. Places that do not update their digital twin will drift into the kind of obscurity that used to be reserved for places that had closed.

The Presence Economy is not a trend. It is what is on the other side of the noise.

It is also, I believe, what the next useful chapter of the internet looks like — one in which the digital layer begins to recognize, catalog, and recommend the physical world not as content to be mined, but as texture to be preserved.

Whether we get there depends on choices being made right now, by people who may not yet know that the choice is theirs.

CLOSING

A Final Note

The analysis in this book draws on a framework developed in the author's graduate research on informational bubbles in digital social networks. That research identified four interlocking levels through which bubbles operate: technological, social, content, and identity. What follows applies that framework — implicitly — to the invisibility of communities and businesses.

What to do, depending on who you are

If you own a brand: complete the self-audit in Chapter 6. Do not delegate it. Search for the business in ChatGPT, Perplexity, and Google's AI Overview. Do this monthly. The structural gaps close in months; the narrative and identity gaps reward those who start early and stay patient.

If you develop marketing strategy: the four-pillar framework in this book can be applied directly. Apply the diagnostic in Chapter 4 to any organization whose category depends on physical presence, map the results to the four kinds of work described in Chapter 5. The work ahead is neither mystical nor opaque. It is architectural, and it begins with diagnosis.

If you work in journalism or research: the phenomenon named in this book deserves more coverage than it is currently receiving. The cultural consequences of algorithmic invisibility are not yet being discussed with the seriousness they merit. Any journalist, scholar, or commentator who takes this on will be early, and early matters.

If you build the tools that shape AI discovery: the decisions being made inside your engineering teams are cultural decisions, even when they do not feel like it. The weighting of sources, the handling of local content, the treatment of small institutions without strong digital representation — these shape which places survive long enough to be found by the next generation. This is not a feature request. It is a responsibility.

If you are simply a reader who cares about what is going on: notice who is mentioned when you ask an AI a question about your town, your county, your region. If your favorite bookstore, your favorite restaurant, your favorite small museum does not appear, that absence is information. The people that matter to you are, in some quiet way, disappearing into a gap that most people have not yet named.

You have named it now.

— Drey Russell · Journalist, researcher, media strategist · April 2026

About the Author

Drey Russell is a journalist, media strategist and researcher. She holds a master's degree in communication, where she defended a thesis on informational bubbles and strategic isolation in digital social networks. Her research focused on the four interlocking levels — technological, social, content, and identity — through which informational membranes form and sustain themselves inside contemporary communication ecosystems. *Algorithmic Invisibility* is the direct application of her master's research to the commercial and cultural challenges facing physical businesses in the age of generative AI.

As a media strategist, she led competitive research and benchmarking to inform national communication campaigns in Brazil — translating behavioral research and market intelligence into positioning strategies for federal institutions, including the Ministry of Tourism, the Ministry of Human Rights and the Government of Rio de Janeiro.

Beyond her strategic work, Russell leads the non-profit organization A+TEIA, spearheading digital literacy initiatives for minority populations and managing cultural and literature festivals that foster community engagement.

In 2026, drawing on the framework developed in this book, she founded Always On — a practice dedicated to the work *Algorithmic Invisibility* describes.

She is currently a fellow in the Lede Program at Columbia University's Graduate School of Journalism, with a focus on computational methods and data reporting.

Bibliography

Aggarwal, P., Murahari, V., Rajpurohit, T., Kalyan, A., Narasimhan, K., & Deshpande, A. (2024). GEO: Generative engine optimization. *Proceedings of the 30th ACM SIGKDD Conference on Knowledge Discovery and Data Mining.*

Benkler, Y. (2006). *The wealth of networks: How social production transforms markets and freedom.* Yale University Press.

Bourdieu, P. (1984). *Distinction: A social critique of the judgement of taste* (R. Nice, Trans.). Harvard University Press. (Original work published 1979)

Bourdieu, P. (1986). The forms of capital. In J. G. Richardson (Ed.), *Handbook of theory and research for the sociology of education* (pp. 241–258). Greenwood Press.

boyd, d. (2014). *It's complicated: The social lives of networked teens.* Yale University Press.

Braga, J. L. (2006). *A sociedade enfrenta sua mídia: Dispositivos sociais de crítica midiática.* Paulus.

Castells, M. (2010). *The rise of the network society* (2nd ed.). Wiley-Blackwell.

Couldry, N., & Hepp, A. (2017). *The mediated construction of reality.* Polity Press.

Crary, J. (2013). *24/7: Late capitalism and the ends of sleep.* Verso.

Gartner. (2024). *Top strategic technology trends for 2025* [Industry report]. Gartner, Inc.

Gillespie, T. (2018). *Custodians of the internet: Platforms, content moderation, and the hidden decisions that shape social media.* Yale University Press.

Google. (n.d.). *Search quality rater guidelines.* Google LLC.

Habermas, J. (1989). *The structural transformation of the public sphere* (T. Burger, Trans.). MIT Press. (Original work published 1962)

Han, B.-C. (2015). *The burnout society* (E. Butler, Trans.). Stanford University Press.

Hepp, A. (2020). *Deep mediatization.* Routledge.

Hjarvard, S. (2013). *The mediatization of culture and society.* Routledge.

Jenkins, H. (2006). *Convergence culture: Where old and new media collide.* NYU Press.

Lopes, M. I. V. de (2014). Mediação e recepção: Algumas reflexões sobre os estudos de recepção no Brasil. *MATRIZes, 8*(1), 65–80.

Manovich, L. (2013). *Software takes command.* Bloomsbury Academic.

Martino, L. M. S. (2014). *Teoria das mídias digitais: Linguagens, ambientes, redes.* Vozes.

Negroponte, N. (1995). *Being digital.* Knopf.

Pariser, E. (2011). *The filter bubble: What the internet is hiding from you.* Penguin Press.

Santos, A. R. S. (2024). *Furar as bolhas: estratégias jornalísticas contra o isolamento de grupos antidemocráticos nas eleições presidenciais brasileiras de 2022 e no 08 de janeiro de 2023* [Master's thesis, Universidade Federal de Sergipe]. Repositório Institucional UFS. https://ri.ufs.br/handle/riufs/20608

Seer Interactive. (2024). *Zero-click search behavior in the age of AI overviews* [Research report].

Sodré, M. (2002). *Antropológica do espelho: Uma teoria da comunicação linear e em rede.* Vozes.

Sunstein, C. R. (2017). *#Republic: Divided democracy in the age of social media.* Princeton University Press.

van Dijck, J. (2013). *The culture of connectivity: A critical history of social media.* Oxford University Press.

Wu, T. (2016). *The attention merchants: The epic scramble to get inside our heads.* Knopf.

Zuboff, S. (2019). *The age of surveillance capitalism: The fight for a human future at the new frontier of power.* PublicAffairs.

www.ingramcontent.com/pod-product-compliance
Lightning Source LLC
LaVergne TN
LVHW011053110826
845149LV00015B/3480

* 9 7 9 8 9 9 5 9 2 0 6 1 8 *